Winkle Pickers & Brothel Creepers

Also by Jill Gower
Elastic Time (Brand New Lino)
Shape of My Life (Ginninderra Press
Garden Delights (Ginninderra Press Pocket Poets)

Edited by Jill Gower
Frost and Fire (Ginninderra Press)
Through the Tunnel (Ginninderra Press)

Jill Gower

Winkle Pickers & Brothel Creepers

for my family
Neil, Tina, Paul, Sacha
Brianna, Zachary and Sam
Alex, Noah and Isla May
and in memory of my mother and father

Winkle Pickers & Brothel Creepers
ISBN 978 1 76041 514 3
Copyright © text Jill Gower 2018
Cover: Belinda Broughton

First published 2018 by
Ginninderra Press
PO Box 3461 Port Adelaide 5015 Australia
www.ginninderrapress.com.au

Contents

Winkle Pickers & Brothel Creepers	7
Happy Valley Days	9
William Torbitt Primary School	13
Street Party	14
Celluloid Hero	15
Before the Baby Boomers	16
Brook Street Nursing Home for Unmarried Mothers, 1958	18
Warm Sunshine & Dribbles of Rain	21
Night Sky	23
Full Moon	24
Poets on *Popeye*	25
The Other Side of the River	26
Tanka	27
Night Shower	28
Skyline	29
Beach Frenzy	30
Infinity	31
Summer Heatwave	32
Love Apple	33
Conquering	34
Maple	35
A Field of Mushrooms	36
Winter Storm	37
Conflict of Seasons	38
A Thing of Beauty	39
The Talking Tree	40
Courtship	41
Bowerbird	42
Chasing Rainbows	43

Stolen — 45

- Stolen — 47
- Anniversary Gift — 49
- Kaleidoscope — 50
- Turn Back the Clock — 51
- Betty & Tom — 52
- Constable's Inspiration — 55
- Spanish Inquisition — 57
- Vincent — 59

Pomegranates of Kandahar — 61

- Pomegranates of Kandahar — 63
- The Kite Runners' Prize — 65
- Flight — 67

The Best of Both Worlds — 69

- Loco-motion — 71
- St Mark's Square — 73
- Red Geraniums — 74
- The Fall of Signor Berenti (alphabetically speaking) — 75
- Kaleidoscope Travels — 76
- Girl on a Train — 77
- Petra's Dilemma — 78
- Fingers — 79
- Pensioner's Half-price Ticket to Nowhere — 80
- Camel train at Victor Harbor — 81
- Lifetime Renal Agreement — 82
- Sign of the Times — 83
- Detour — 84
- The Rooms — 86
- The Pine Table — 87
- Terrorist Attacks — 89
- Ode to a Combustion Heater — 92
- Bridgewater Town — 93

Acknowledgements — 97

Winkle Pickers
& Brothel Creepers

Happy Valley Days

1. Happy Valley Days

we ran wild in the allotments
climbed the tree with good footholds
looked out over our surrounds
watching for the approach of enemies
we fished in the stream below
with homemade nets on sticks
catching tiddlers and roach
that darted silver in the current
sometimes we whittled bows and arrows
from branches of shrubs
and divided into groups of
cowboys and indians
whooping through the woods

2. Cubby House

the building site
at the end of our street
became our playground
we built houses
out of oddments
of bricks and wood
and made pretend cups of tea
from the nearby tap
re-enacted our parents' lives
played happy families

3. Tall Poppies

we staggered on stilts made from
green & gold Tate & Lyle syrup tins
punched with holes and threaded with string
up and down the street we went
lurching and overbalancing
falling to the kerb in fits of giggles

4. Hop Scotch & Five Stones

on the pavement
we chalked coloured numbers
jumped and hopped
like kangaroos in the outback
or squatted in groups
to flick five stones
backwards and forwards
on the backs of our hands
trying hard to keep the balance
and not let them fall

5. Marbles

hours were spent
rolling marbles
along street gutters
as our conquests
jangled in prized cotton bags
that sagged heavily
from the safety of wrists
the blood marble
was the most prized of all
milky white with red streaks
leaching through
if you lost a blood
it was the worst thing
the more you won
the bigger your reputation

6. Skipping

red jelly
yellow jelly
red jelly
yellow jelly
tongues so twisted
that we fell laughing
tripped on the rope
and were OUT

7. Shadow Play

when darkness fell
and only a little light
seeped around the doors
and into the room
fingers and fists
made shadows on the wall
rabbits with long ears
and birds with wings like eagles
we made our own movie shows
in those good old days

William Torbitt Primary School

On the end of the back row stands Mr Aston
our class teacher, a kind man, very solemn
when he announced to our class in 1952
'The king is dead, long live the queen.'
The photographer has positioned us
into four rows. I'm sitting third from the left

cross-legged on the dry summer grass
unusually demure, hands folded
pretty dress and neat pigtails.
Edna Spooner, further along the row
was a vivacious girl who made up stories
about everybody else.

Next to me is Anita who lived
across the road. She would wave to her mother
and call goodbye till her mother was out of sight.
Then Patricia Manners
a large, untidy girl, whose conduct
was not so good as her name implied.

Behind me, centre of row, stands Christine.
She was my friend for a long time
until we had a minor argument
at Sunday school. She flushed my Bible
leaving me to fish the soggy pages
out of the loo.

Missing from this photograph is Robert Smith.
A bomb fell on his house, leaving a huge crater in the back garden.

Street Party

I'm looking at an old photo
of a street party
taken when I was about twelve
Elizabeth is twenty-five years old
& has just been crowned
Queen of England

there are street parties
all over Britain
celebrating her coronation
& even though
the photo is black & white
I can recognise my childhood home

remember the low curved wall
at the front of our house
the big bay windows
next door's car, a Triumph Mayflower,
sits in the shade of a tree
in the June sunshine

trestle tables are pushed up
along one side of the road
laden with sandwiches, cakes & drinks
all the kids from the street sit at the tables
the mothers stand behind them
not the fathers, they are at work

two of the older girls
wave huge Union Jacks over our heads
& everyone is happy for our new queen

Celluloid Hero

she lit candles
every week
in homage
to her hero
of the fifties

he came to the screen
like a golden Apollo
left just as suddenly
driving his silver Porsche
into oblivion

she scattered rose petals
as a symbol
of her love
lit candles
placed them in a circle

a shrine of mirrors
framed by glossies of her idol
sat high upon a ledge
could be viewed
from every angle
and when she kneeled before it

the candles flickered
in the breeze
of her movement
candles that soon
spluttered and died
just like Jimmy Dean

Before the Baby Boomers

I found new freedom
in the late nineteen fifties
with Elvis and Bill Haley
as I jived my teenage years away
twisting my body to the beat
layers of flouncing petticoats.
long ponytail flying

In a café with friends
the drop of a coin sent
my favourite tune belting
out of the jukebox
white light glared from neon tubes
the chrome Italian coffee machine gleamed
and hissed steam into frothy cappuccinos.

In the pubs on Saturday nights
teddy boys in drainpipe trousers
shuffled suede brothel creepers
across the parquet dance floor.
Girls in winkle pickers
pouted sexily like Brigitte Bardot
and drooled over James Dean posters.

A few years later
I listened to the Beatles and Stones
passed joints and drank cheap Bordeaux
with a new group of friends.
The genius of Hendrix and his guitar
pounded in our ears while we debated
the Vietnam war and the tragic demise of JFK.

But at the pubs and clubs
rock band groupies
with slender legs and miniskirts,
swung their straight hair
looked through ink-lined eyes
and gyrated hips at long-haired musicians
as they wondered who they would sleep with that night.

Brook Street Nursing Home for Unmarried Mothers, 1958

(for my son, Neil)

It's around midnight
when my labour pains start,
my parents packing me
and my small bag
into the family A40
and we race
through dark quiet streets
to the gloomy old building
built in the late eighteen hundreds.

The entrance is dimly lit
a desk with a bell to ring
and a few wooden chairs.
My father's face is pale
my mother's full of worry
as a nurse appears, curtly deals
with some paperwork
picks up my bag
and tells them both to go home.

I am led down a corridor
into a labour room
old white tiles, garish lighting
and a narrow bed
in the middle of the room.
Unfamiliar sounds of women birthing
and smells of antiseptic and the
fustiness of this old building
frighten me. I feel very alone.

It's two months
past my seventeenth birthday
and my school exams.
My labour pains
now more regular
shock me into the reality
of what is about to happen.

The midwives are matter-of-fact
devoid of emotion
crisp as their stiff
starched hats and collars.
They perform their procedures briskly,
and appear to be immune
to my feelings and fear.

My son is born
and immediately taken away.
But they bring him back
when it's time to bottle feed him.
They take him away
then bring him back
every day, several times a day
for the next ten days
that I must stay in this place.

When it is time for me to leave
my parent's faces are masks
as they try to conceal their own pain.
My son will be adopted
within the next few days.
He is given to me to hold
in a final goodbye hug,
and I am left numb
as I follow my parents
out through the dingy hall
without my baby.

Warm Sunshine
& Dribbles of Rain

Night Sky

daylight has been
snuffed out
by dusk

cobalt blue
replaced
with inky-black

night sky
is littered
with stars

while a thin
crescent of moon
is pasted

in space
and in another place
someone else

is looking at
all of this
at
    exactly
        the same time
            as me

Full Moon

you are the silver coin
in the man's blue serge pocket
you are the shiny button
on the lapel of a London pearly king
you are a honeydew melon
on a market stall
you are a balloon
whose helium never runs out

but a moon is a moon
and there you are
beaming away
as you circle around the earth
your brilliant light flashing across the world
inspiring poets everywhere
to write moon poems

Poets on *Popeye*

the peal of cathedral bells
shivers blossoms

and echoes across the white shell
of the theatre

to the river
a curling silver serpent

alive with rowing eights
and the blue and white *Popeye*

as it chugs to the weir past water reeds
where birds nest in the safety of dusk

laughing poets recline
and listen to poetry that flows

as gently as the Torrens itself
they lean over the side of the boat

trail fingers at gliding black swans
who communicate their delight

in guttural sounds of pleasure
as they majestically swim alongside

it is hard to choose
whether to listen to the reader

or the swans

The Other Side of the River

(haibun)

The sun is shining on the other side of the river, up in the sky and down in the water. It wiggles a bit with the gentle flowing motion, sending out prisms of light. Green moss on the bank is vivid, matched by the leaves of weeping willows that bow their branches gently down to the water, creating a natural hanging garden. Tucked into the bank, half out of view is an old wooden rowing boat, one oar sticking out sideways between the willow leafy branches.

> tiny wrens
> flit from tree to bank
> to wooden boat

A black swan folds her young cygnets under her wing, pushing them with her bright red beak, keeping them close to her. They stay near the bank. Later they swim regally upstream, circles of water rippling behind the tiny cygnets. A green dragonfly skitters along the surface, sunlight glistening on its wings. It hums as it searches for small insects.

Two ducks are also diving for food, tails vertical in the air. Following each other they swim on, leaving corrugated V shapes in their wake, their loud quacks echoing through the trees. A moorhen swims serenely past, an ibis paddles in the shallows.

On the other side of the river, shadows are darkening as day fades. An owl screeches in the distance. Trees appear to change shape and colour as the moon is chased behind a cloud.

> the moon
> dances a samba
> with the stars

Tanka

dangling above
the midnight blue of sea
between smoky clouds
a shred of moon dances gently
on an invisible string

Night Shower

the moon has been sideswiped
by a cloud

leaving it
with a dent in its side

the stars
have been doused by rain

turning the sky
into a midnight-blue quilt

flying foxes
fold their wings

like umbrellas waiting
to be unfurled

an owl blinks away raindrops
his eyelids like windscreen wipers

a moth flutters
blind around a street light

Skyline

high above the city buildings
a slow sky ballet
as, dressed in tutus of white clouds,
the latticed booms
of mechanical cranes
dance a *pas de deux*
lift and swing
lift and swing
in their slow *ports de bras*
against a sapphire backdrop

Beach Frenzy

at the beach
wind gusts send

grainy sand
flying into faces

plastic buckets are blown
like feathers across the sand

beach balls lift up
& plonk down again into the sea

seagulls circle
raucously above

debris skitters
along the promenade

bunting on the kiosk
whiplashes the air

café umbrellas
are quickly rolled

& plastic chairs pushed
under tables

people run for shelter
in a mass frenzy

while seemingly unaware
a Labrador dog paddles in the ocean

Infinity

On one of those five-mile sandy beaches
I sat before an endless ocean
And gazed at the black velvet sky
Scattered with a myriad glittering stars.

I thought about infinity
About all the matter that was floating
Somewhere above my head in that dark space.

Life forms on planets watching me down here.
Celestial bodies of the dead perhaps
Embracing my mother and my grandparents
In some form or other not visible to my eye.

I thought about laser beams slicing the sky
And emails – all those little words
Floating in space; unread poems
Erased from the computer, gone where?

And satellites on their way to the moon
Orbiting the earth in never-ending circles

A shooting star fizzed across the sky
As I watched and contemplated
And felt the absolute peace of solitude
Just a minute dot in this vast universe.

Summer Heatwave

the heat is oppressive
and never-ending
it has arrived
with northerly winds
and scorching days
that have dried
the grass brown
dust rains down
coats eyes and hair and skin
'we're having a heatwave,
a tropical heatwave'
sang Marilyn Monroe
back in the fifties
and it's been about that long
since we had such a spell
the chopper
is a constant buzz
as it circles overhead
scanning for bushfires
in the garden a single bird
cries a parched call
through its half-open beak
a sapphire sky
turns to pale blue
trees dance a slow waltz
that quickens to a tarantella
as branches splinter to the ground
dried brown gum leaves
whirl and spin
litter lawns and footpaths
in a crackly jigsaw
a yellow eeriness hangs overhead

Love Apple

fiery red temptress
testicular globe
hanging sexily
from pale green stem
plump and succulent
with gentle curves
and crevices
waiting to be stroked
and sucked
by my eager tongue

I gently remove you
from your spidery
umbilical cord
embrace your juices
with a shake of salt
douse your skin
with virgin olive oil
take a first bite
to release your
summery sweetness

Conquering

A stroll through an English park
highlights autumn colours against a pale blue sky.
Mosaic patterns of leaves crunch beneath my feet
everywhere horse chestnut trees
their blooming white candle flowers
pushing between the seven-fingered leaves.
Spiky pale green cases have split
to reveal glossy brown chestnuts or conkers
that lie on the ground like jewels.
I remember children filling their pockets till they bulged
racing home to prepare for battle
piercing holes through centres
threading them with string.
A tight knot on one side of the hole
and a good length of string at the other.
Battles would commence between two players
one winding string around his hand
and holding the nut still at the right height,
the striker attempting to hit his opponent's conker
over and over again with his own.
Strings would get tangled
as the two conkers twisted and smashed together.
The player whose conker remained intact
was the winner, but the game was over
for the player whose conker was split.
Continuing through the park to a grassy clearing
I stand and watch some Canadian geese
see the brush of a squirrel as it rushes for shelter
but I'm still thinking about the game of conkers
and I smile to myself as I remember how I too
used to play this game so many years ago.

Maple

in my garden, the maple sways
this way and that
as the breeze takes it
it's still a sapling at two years old
but it sure knows how to dress
for the autumn festival of leaves
blushing as the passers-by
admire its coat of many colours

A Field of Mushrooms

i wandered into a field one damp and misty winter's day. not sure why. funny how the honey-coloured cows barely paused in their cud-chewing routine. they turned their beautiful eyes limpidly in my direction, that's all. moo moo said i in my sturdy shoes long red coat woolly hat and mittens. a twitch of their heads maybe at this odd sight, but no not even a modicum of curiosity. between their feet amongst cow pats the first clusters of mushrooms. a nuclear explosion from underground. clouds of agaricus campestris. field mushrooms. scanning the field like captain cook eyes wide open now i see them everywhere huddled together growing rapidly before my eyes. they were chattering shyly to each other these cheap cousins of exquisite truffles found in *les bois de France*. pulled one from the ground held it gently in my hands studied its delicate paleness. its soft creamy texture. upside-down it's a contrast of dark chocolate umbrella rib supports and cappuccino on a stalk. i took it home cooked it ate it for my breakfast. delicious.

Winter Storm

rain sheeting down
filling creeks to overflowing
swelling oceans
giant waves battering shorelines
eroding beaches
threatening homes

gale-force winds
rage through old gum trees
that sway like young saplings
in a struggle for their lives
while others thunder across roads
onto roofs or cars

air is icy cold
rain becoming hail
racketing on buildings and gardens
where it gathers like snow
settles on footpaths, gardens
windscreens

but such cold beauty
takes my breath away
until the magic melts

Conflict of Seasons

late winter
warm sunshine and dribbles of rain
trees and plants in confusion
hard push of jonquils
through still-warm earth
small white flowers budding
while the crimson leaves of the young maple
unwilling to let go
cling precariously to fragile branches
only the soursobs seem certain
    that winter
        is around the next corner

A Thing of Beauty

emerging
through grey garden gravel
a spear
that every day
pushes higher
until it bends
beneath its own weight

an asparagus head perhaps
but no, the stalk is too long
I can't work out what it is
and warn everyone
coming to my door
to walk around it
for its own safety

but defying gravel
and gravity
drought and flood
delicate pink buds unfurl
revealing in all its beauty
a wild hyacinth orchid

The Talking Tree

against the side fence
of my back garden
on a warm breezy day
a giant ash reaches out its arms
as if to draw me in
whispering to come and sit in its shade
watch the kaleidoscope patterns
of blue sky shimmering between leaves

on strong windy days
the tree seems disgruntled
rustling noisily and whipping up a frenzy
stay indoors today, be safe, it shouts
as a bough crashes to the ground
a thud that has me running
while the continuous rain
leaves pools of tears on leaves

some days
the ash offers up a spokesperson
a pigeon to coo soft words to me
parrots screaming obscenities
and galahs puffing out their rosy chests
ululating constantly
as they canoodle together
while blackbirds
gargle the sweetest words of all

Courtship

a monotonous cooing
brings me to the kitchen window
and on the circle of pavers
a speckle-collared turtle dove
stands on red spindly legs
his small white head and tail
touch the ground in unison with his call
he is puffed up with importance
mottled wings catch the sun
and gleam with blue and green iridescence
his chest a delicate rose pink

soon she alights beside him
to begin their dance of love
bobbing heads as they circle together
they feign retreat as they move apart
a sudden flurry when he lands on her back
soon he dismounts
circles her a few laps
stops and spreads his tail in a beautiful fan
in homage to his partner

they parade together down the garden path
pecking the ground as they go
just another happy couple

Bowerbird

You Hugh Hefner of the bird world
working away to coax your love
into your ground floor apartment.
It's ostentatious interior
shines with jewels of coloured glass
and a scattering of flowers and berries.
You are the designer of bling
peeping coyly from within,
the architect of pillars and thatched roofs
built to please the girl of your dreams.
You create optical illusions
to hold your mate's attention,
keep her in your sights
but your amazing electric blue eyes
are not enough to seal the deal,
it's your real estate she's really after.
Now, shyly, she's inside your bachelor pad
crouching, half-hidden in the grass
while you strut your stuff
an elaborate dance to make sure she stays,
fluffing your feathers, running back and forth
emitting strange vocals.
Four times you perform this manic dance
but still she dashes off to visit the bower next door
to see if it is more to her taste.
Let's hope you haven't done your dash.
You'll have to wait a while
to see if your artistry and your sexy dance
will entice her beneath your wing.

Chasing Rainbows

I want to swim
in the silvery lake of the moon
roll on my back
and worship the stars

I want to run naked
in the valleys of your dreams
and climb the mountains
to your heart

I want to inhale
the scent from your skin
as I lie in your arms
counting *my* dreams

I want to taste the salt
on your body
as we make love
in the heat of the day

I want to chase the rainbow
that arcs above our heads
soak up its iridescence
through my eyes

I want to share
my life with you

Stolen

Stolen

she's three years old or so
peeping anxiously
from her mother's skirts
when they come to remove her
to steal her
from her family
her land
and everything familiar
her skin is the wrong colour
not light
not dark
a beautiful colour
she should be brought up by white people
in white people's ways
her mother is told

never mind that she is happy
well-fed and clean
this is the white man's law
she should speak English
not that Aboriginal babble
that no one else can understand

it is forty-five years
before she sees her younger sister again
and her mother has died
anyway
what was the point of saying 'sorry'
back in 2008
when eight years further on
children even now
are still being removed
from their communities
risking a second stolen generation

Anniversary Gift

On my bookshelf,
three porcelain shells

glazed with pastel flashes
of pink lemon and purple

threaded with delicate veins
of exquisite gold lustre.

Green splotches are seaweed stains
in the whorls and crannies

where sea creatures
might have lived,

my gift to my mother and father
on the anniversary

of their golden wedding.
Fragile, like they were

in those last years
before the shells became mine.

Kaleidoscope

(for my father)

fragments
of a past life
shaking
and falling
into different patterns

all the pieces
and shapes
still there somewhere
but every movement
every fall
reveals a new pattern
of the same life

dementia
is like a shadow
that envelops the moon

or a jigsaw puzzle
that does not quite fit
and some pieces
lost for ever

Turn Back the Clock

(for Charmaine)

stop the clock
turn back two years
just to be safe

stop the clock
spin the hands backwards
to how she was

before she learnt
of the cancer
travelling through her body

turn the clock back
before blood tests and scans
chemo and radiotherapy

became daily outings
and a good day was rare
turn the clock back

to before she lay helpless in bed
morphine easing the pain
every hour of the day

stop, please stop the clock

Betty & Tom

1. Princess

'She's a little princess,'
says Betty who lives next door
as she smiles at my baby.
Betty smokes umpteen cigarettes
each day
& sits in front of her TV
a cask of port at her side.
The smoke wafts into the airless room
& mingles with fumes
from the old wood stove.
'Our princess had polio,'
says Betty,
'& wore callipers
& every day
my Tom carried her in his arms
one mile to the train station
for treatment in the city.'
Tom grins, lifts his glass of amber
passes a few comments on the local football
& his greyhounds out in the yard.
Betty tipsily adjusts her Alice hairband
as she reminisces & hands me an apple pie
fresh from the wood stove.
She has a heart of gold, old Betty.

I carry my beautiful princess home.

2. Till Death Us Do Part

The day Betty died
the house went silent.
Every day before that was yelling
& screaming abuse at each other.
But no sound came
from the house next door
once the ambulance had left.
Now Tom was never far
from his cask of old tawny
until his gout got so painful
he could hardly move.
So after a while when he began to feel better
he put his life back into the local footy club
training the players
massaging their limbs with liniment
just as he had done in previous years
until they could stand it no more.
During the day he walked his greyhound, Suzie,
or took her to the races when they were on.
One night the fox took two of his chickens
& the next he was waiting with his shotgun.
The fox was crafty
two more hens & Tom gave up.

Something in him died with Betty.

3. The Declining Years of Tom

Betty had gone.
The greyhound stopped barking,
the fox had taken the chickens.
His daughter wanted to fly him to Melbourne
to visit his favourite grandson
a successful chef who would cook him nice food.
Now Tom fell over, often,
in the house
in the garden
on the street.
Once he dripped blood
across my new white carpet
as I tried to dress his wounds.
He developed Parkinson's disease
& went into residential care.
One day, towards the end
I visited him in hospital
took the spoon from the nurse
who was shovelling yoghurt
into his mouth
at the speed of light

& gave him back some dignity.

Constable's Inspiration

(Suffolk, England)

I know Constable country,
having lived not far from the mosaic scenery
that was his inspiration.
He grew up at Flatford Mill
where his father milled corn,
and next door was Willy Lott's cottage
featured in *The Hay Wain*,
one of his six-foot paintings
for which the king of France
once awarded him a gold medal.

I have a small print on my wall;
the stillness of the river,
a cloud-filled sky, the cottage,
a small dog waiting on the riverbank.
Horses drinking as they rest from pulling the hay wagon
across the rich green of fields.

The Lock, another of his huge paintings,
shows a small boat that has just passed,
the boatman attending
to the water levels at Flatford Mill.

I've wandered the fields
near the flat pond of the river,
stood at his father's flour mill,
and visited Willy Lott's cottage.

I followed Constable's footsteps.
He would have walked here with Maria, his wife,
chatting about her alienated family,
their unhappiness at his poverty,
and refusal to attend the wedding.

When Maria died,
after only twelve years of marriage,
Constable wore black for the rest of his life
his heart as dark as the clouds he painted.

Spanish Inquisition

Picasso in his cubist state
painted lopsided bodies
unusual forms and sizes
with geometric shapes for heads
and eyes at different heights.
Cyclops (if he'd visited) with his one eye
in the middle of his forehead
would have found it tricky
to view the world through his armpits.

Salvador Dali's deranged images
women blossoming from trees
with arms of spreading branches
Jesus burning in hell flames
shedding tears of blood
from his wooden cross.
Sculptures of giant floppy watches
that showed his propensity for time
or lack of it.

Gaudi designed gingerbread houses
vanilla iced buildings
that waved and curled.
His cathedral masterpiece
has ill-fated turtles bearing the weight
of pillars on their backs
squashed in an eternity of oppression.

Were they mad, these Spanish artists
or geniuses, creating brilliant works of art?

What happened to more gentle images
fields of poppies
or cornflowers
bright amongst the wheat
and picnics for two in forest glades?

Vincent

(for Tina)

when Vincent
sets up his easel
in the field of sunflowers
takes out his brushes
squeezes tubes of colour
into his palette
does he think of death?

dramatic colour
becomes his expression of emotion
brilliant splashes
of scarlet poppies
purple iris and yellow sunflowers
creations of beauty
and happiness

when he paints
starry nights
beneath dark skies
does he think of his
two unhappy marriages?
or does he see only the beauty
of the night?

depression and fits of epilepsy
turn to madness
he chases his friend
with an open razor
but instead cuts off
part of his own ear
and gives it to a prostitute
an unwelcome gift
from which she recoils

and not much later
still a young man, he shoots himself
his last words
'the sadness will last forever'

Pomegranates of Kandahar

Pomegranates of Kandahar

Afghan girl
takes her children
takes her few belongings
all that she can carry
always running
to a better place

runs and runs
comes full circle
back to Kandahar
city of pomegranates
shiny blushing skins
encasing countless red cells

she recalls the taste
of the sweet and sour love fruit
each bead unique
each red and crunchy
with juices that colour lips
and teeth red
oozing down chins

like blood running
from the mouth
the blood of afghans
injured in wars
the blood of afghans
running over minefields
the blood of Afghan women
stoned to death for
someone else's crimes

love fruit
hate fruit

all this she remembers
from her childhood
nothing has changed

The Kite Runners' Prize

(From *The Kite Runner* by Khaled Hosseini)

1. How to Make a Kite

First visit the bazaar
to buy bamboo glue and paper.
Shave the bamboo to make
the centre cross spans
then cut the tissue paper
so the kite can dip and rise.
Feed hundreds of feet of string
through a mixture of tar
ground glass and glue
and hang between trees to dry
and lastly wind it around a wooden peg.

2.

Before the rule of Taliban
eager boys
flooded Kabul streets
the crunch of winter snow
beneath their feet.

Like exotic birds
colourful kites crammed the sky
gliding and spinning
slicing and sweeping
looping the loop.

The boys played by the rules
cut their rival's kites in a frenzy
watched them spiral down
shooting stars
with brilliant colours
and rippling tails.

Impatient runners
fingers bleeding
from sharp glassy string
jammed streets
the crowd chanting
'cut him cut him'
as music blared from rooftops.

Out of control
the kites whirled and fell
became tangled in tree branches
or crumpled in a blaze of colour
in a neighbour's yard.

The last kite to fall wins the prize
the runner holding it high
in bloodied hands
before passing it
to the triumphant flyer.

Flight

Hungary, September 2015

across vast tracts of land
and treacherous oceans
crammed into ramshackle boats
they flee
desperate refugees
asylum seekers
in their thousands
the aged who must be carried
the children who stumble
the babies in arms
the women and men who must be strong
for all of them
they are weary in a way we have never known
as they cling to hope
hungry thirsty exhausted
halted by tear gas and barbed wire boundaries
built far too quickly
rejection again and again
forced by barbaric soldiers
to run from their own beloved country
or face mutilation rape death
to beg and plead for their lives
now in a peaceful country
still again they are defeated

The Best of Both Worlds

Loco-motion

(Milan to Parma, 2013)

the man on the train
sat down, got up, sat down
the man on the train stood up
rummaged in his case
for a sheet of plastic
spread it over his seat
sat down, got up
straightened it and sat for a while.

the man on the train
stood up, reached for his case
pulled it down to the seat
took out a drawstring bag
hung it on a hook behind his seat
returned his case to the luggage rack
sat down, stood up
adjusted his drawstring bag
and sat down again

the man on the train
stood up, pulled down his drawstring bag
took out his mobile phone
hung up his bag
sat down, stood up
put his phone in his pocket
folded up his plastic sheet very carefully
put it back in his case

sat down, stood up
took out his phone and dialled
went out into the corridor
put his phone in his pocket
came back, sat down, stood up
put his phone back in his bag

the man on the train
took out his ticket, held it in his hand
sat down, stood up
hitched up his pants
put his ticket in his pocket
sat down, stood up
hitched up his pants again
went to the corridor
put his ticket in the waistband of his trousers
came back and sat down

the train neared my station
I stood up, sat down, stood up
pulled down my case
sat down, stood up
pushed my case into the corridor
left the train and the man
who stood up, sat down, stood up
looking out of the window

St Mark's Square

(for Valda)

the small orchestra played lively tunes
in the sunshine
and pigeons ran like ants
between the chairs and tables
greedy for dropped crumbs
I sipped my freshly squeezed orange juice
approximately ten dollars' worth
plus cover charge
but was told l had the privilege of the view
and the music
(which stopped just after I was seated)
the ice came free, with tongs

the square was full of tourists
milling in all directions
just like the pigeons
but the facade of St Mark's
took my breath away
with its beauty

arcades of shops
filled the other three sides of the square
the beautiful fourteenth-century clock tower
was imposing
but some cheap clothing stalls in front of the basilica
were a reality check
while the sun began to bake me

I paid my bill, an even bigger reality cheque
just as the band struck up again

Red Geraniums

(Italy)

brilliant red geraniums
lie bleeding in the sun
against the white skin
of a Mediterranean wall

the wounded sit
in terracotta beds
being tended carefully
by silver-haired matriarchs
in black dresses

The Fall of Signor Berenti (alphabetically speaking)

Albert Berenti came down eventually
fell grotesquely, heavily, into jeopardy
kneeling low, moaning noisily
objecting pathetically
queasily rallied, stood tentatively
understandably vague
was X-rayed, yowling zealously

Kaleidoscope Travels

I hold the brightly coloured tube to my eye
and squint, as green shapes fall into Tuscan valleys
but just a blink reveals the brown River Thames
between historic buildings. I turn the cylinder
and watch as the patterns change to dazzling colours
fluttering and falling with Gaudi brilliance
a configuration of constantly changing mosaic shapes
that soon become the vivid yellow of a Barcelona sun
that shakes to hot fiery flamenco reds.
Now, shadowy forms of grey on blue reveal minarets
silhouetted against an Istanbul sky
before a slight turn shows shimmering belly dancers
swirling to an imagined rhythm
before settling to muted reds and gold cathedral shapes
painted windows forming amazing coloured glass reflections

Girl on a Train

Across the aisle she sat
on the city bound train
a young dark-skinned girl
Bob Marley dreads
lips polished purple
her nostril pierced
with silver ring
dark fathomless eyes stared ahead
as her blue-jeaned leg with rainbow boot
tapped out the rhythm of her heart

Petra's Dilemma

(Seville, Spain)

Petra didn't have a window in her room
it was a cell, she said
I had a window
but I didn't have a bath
Petra had a bath
but no window
and she had a proper wash basin
I had a window but
only a flat basin
that held an inch or two of water
Petra didn't have a window
she told me constantly
but she did have lovely orange walls
and a nice round wooden table
I had yellow and green tiles on my walls
very lurid and unattractive
and a very small table
she also had hot water in the shower
and mine was barely warm
and I had a hard bed and pillow
but at least I had a window
Petra didn't

Fingers

She sat across from me on the train
as it left Euston station,
hands crossed neatly in lap
her age about forty-five.
I noticed her fingers
quite long and slender
pale with smooth skin
unwrinkled, no blemishes
moles or age spots.
Nails filed and shapely
painted with pale pink varnish.
She held her train ticket
ready for the inspector.
I noticed a tattoo,
a ring, delicate, patterned.
It transfixed me
and I wanted to ask
what made her do it
what it meant.
But she got to her feet
as the train halted at the station
stepped onto the platform
the doors closing
on my unspoken question

Pensioner's Half-price Ticket to Nowhere

Her ill-fitting false teeth
click clack in her mouth
in time to the train's rhythmic beat.
Her look is of disinterest
as she watches the countryside
race by at high speed,
a blend of green paddocks
red roofs
a few sheep and cows.

It's all a blur
to her fading eyes.
She can't really remember her destination
or even if there is one.
Her daughter put her on the train
and will no doubt meet her
on her return journey.

She takes a peppermint from her bag
pops it in her mouth.
Her teeth are stilled for that short time.

The train slows down.
She wonders if she is meant to get off
but remains in her seat
heart pounding with uncertainty.
The train resumes its journey.
Her teeth continue their clicking
as she waits for her half-price journey to end
so she can return to the safety
of her own small world.

Camel train at Victor Harbor

I walk across
the wooden causeway
warm ocean slurping at pylons

below my feet water-reeds dance
as a single fish weaves
in a frenzy of bubbles

I reach the mainland
where waves are a soft caress
at the edge of the sand

four camels rest
their legs folded clumsily
beneath them

soft doe-like eyes
framed by long curly lashes
lazily watch punters

then unfurling spindly legs
the camels stand awkwardly
yellow teeth bared

as they moan and bawl
with the physical effort
like Olympic weightlifters in action

the waiting riders scramble for a hold
and seated behind a hump
laugh at their own exertions

the driver leads the train across the sand
camels tethered as they shamble
and sway, ropey tails swishing at flies

Lifetime Renal Agreement

I'd just seen a sign outside a building
on the way to the city
'Lifetime Renal Agreement'.
Something for me to follow up, I thought,
an attractive proposition,
what with only having one kidney and all.
So I got quite excited and thought
this could mean a longer and healthier life maybe
so it would be worth signing up
if it wasn't too costly.
I went into the office to ascertain
the finer details of this contract
did it include check-ups
and blood tests for example
but paled when I was told
that what the sign actually said
was Lifetime *Rental* Agreement!

Sign of the Times

at the side of the Main North Road
the hand-painted sign reads 'baby sale'
& conjures up pictures
of delectable babies
arranged on lace-covered trestles
pastel-clad
in their best bib & tucker
peachy-faced
gummy smiles
arms & legs moving like rotor blades
as they demonstrate
their cuteness
asking to be cuddled
asking to be loved

flashing past the sign I giggle
& hope the sale
is for clothes
& baby wear
and not for pre-loved babies
but you can't be sure
these days…

Detour

If it's not bad enough
that I'm driving in unknown territory
that I've got lost already, twice
and just when I think I'm almost
at my destination
there is a council detour sign
the usual mustard background
black letters and an arrow
which I dutifully follow
turning left at the next street
then another sign
instructing me to go straight ahead
confusion is overriding
when the road turns into a T-junction
where now, I ask myself?
in the distance I can just see
the top of another sign
as I come up over a hill
so I keep going until the arrow
tells me to turn left again
It's a puzzle – I'm sure that's
the way I just came from
are they having a laugh?
I turn left as I'm lost anyway
keep going to the end of the street
and I'm back where I began
I've had enough so I'm going home
but five hundred yards up the road
is yet another detour sign!

sick of going in circles
I make a detour of my own
head to the nearest café
de-stress with a long black

The Rooms

the walls of my house
are blank pages
I would paint a stanza
       in each room

delicate brushstrokes
for nature poems
big bold splashes
       for political comment

in the bedroom
it would be
a poem about love
       and caring

and in the kitchen
scenes through the window
birds or flowers
       or ripe scarlet tomatoes

and everywhere
friezes in little squares
       sequences of haiku

the final stanza
could be a fresco
       applied with care

each room a different poem
the whole house
       a book of poems

The Pine Table

it was the one
I knew as soon as I saw it
in the carpenter's workroom
pinewood with four sturdy square-cut legs
to support panels of pale blonde wood
that would mellow to warm honeyed tones
as it seasoned

I stroked the beautiful knots
the swirls and shapes
that conjured up all sorts of images
one a micro head of a fox
another an eye watching over me

a few weeks later
a fondue night with friends
the flame accidentally
burning the surface
an attractive dark etching
now a lovely reminder of that evening

how many family meals
and dinner parties with friends
has it hosted
how much laughter
and how many tears have been shed
over cups of coffee
or a glass of wine

these days it is covered with papers
articles not yet read
recipes still to be tried
unfinished crossword puzzles

and more than thirty-five years later
I still marvel at its knots and shades of caramel

Terrorist Attacks

oh! loathsome creature
you are a horror movie
your six feet clad
in filthy boots

you get your rocks off
when you are immersed
in dirt and grease
infesting kitchens
is your favourite pleasure

your body looks
like polished wood
but all I see is your dark
brown crustiness

my skin creeps
when I see you
crawl in my house
your antennae
waving salutations
like anti-aircraft missiles
you repulse me

I imagine you scuttling
in the dark of night
you nocturnal creature
that runs from light

I shudder that
you may have
gate crashed
my bedroom
made it a torture chamber
you the torturer
me on the rack

you are voracious
your hunger never sated
in my cupboards, you lurk
seeking every last crumb

you inhabit
the squalid world
of garbage bins
searching for
a mouldy
treat amongst
the plastic
and the papers

prisoners
in filthy cells
have been forced
to munch you
in order to survive
I'd rather die

I have seen you
from the safety
of my armchair
scurry from the
fire's waiting logs

I'd like to see you
roast in hell flames
but I find another weapon

I squeeze the trigger
keep on squeezing
watch the fine mist work
until you the terrorist
are lying on your back
all six legs are stiff and still

you kamikaze roach

Ode to a Combustion Heater

I saw you across the other side of the room
leaning nonchalantly against the hearth.
The fire flared in your eyes
as they flickered in my direction
smoke began to curl from your mouth.
I was drawn towards the heat
of your hard, black body.
My hand reached out, touching your ebony skin
burnt by your hot passion.
You were looking at me with your glass eye
watching me shiver with delight.
I sat by your feet as you vented your heat over me.
I'd never felt such warmth before.
You waited for me to stoke you up
for the flame in your belly to be rekindled.
But I confess, smoke got in my eyes
I didn't see the flame had gone from yours.
It didn't even last through that first night.
I've got a handle on you now though
can see your blackened heart was only made of wood.
No problem, you're a bit square for me after all.

Bridgewater Town

(after Geoff Goodfellow)

Bridgewater
      you are constantly changing
in summer you are bushfires
      and hot winds
in winter you are rain
      and icy hail

you have a main street
that runs straight past the deli
      and the local pub
      and a football oval
that is flooded every winter

you have parallel streets called
1st   2nd   and 3rd avenues
but they are not the big avenues
      of New York New York
they lead instead to the other side of town
where all roads lead to roads
      that begin with the letter O

you are individual
not a country town nor metropolitan
you are the best of both worlds
      the country locals
that whisper on every corner
      and the city migrants
that stand aloof

    Bridgewater
you can feel proud
of your rural surroundings
your running creek
    and your European trees
and even though you are a
small community
    you are diverse
because if you are not
a hippie
    in a velvet skirt and leggings
or a footballer
    in a pair of skimpy shorts
if you are not into Pilates
    or tennis
or walking the Heysen trail

if you are not a writer
    or a painter
a potter   or a priest

    if Ross the local butcher
doesn't give you flak
    and a ready conversation
then it's doubtful that
    this is the place for you

in autumn
>	the leaves are jewels
of claret and rust and gold
>	as they weave a crispy carpet underfoot

I came to you in the seventies
when land was for the picking
now there are few blocks left
>	for the builders to fill
>>	with their bricks and mortar
their landscaped gardens

Bridgewater   you have shamed yourself
your public transport system is archaic
you closed the railway station
no more Red Hens
>	no more Overland to Melbourne
>>	or Bluebird to the mount

you allowed discontented neighbours
to stop Sunday music sessions
at the pub
>	no jazz
>>	or blues
>>>	or rock n roll

your retirement village is the size
>	of a postage stamp
where is your gym
>	your public swimming pool
your police station
>	even your fish shop has gone

but you've got me dreaming
        and when I retire
I'll have time to smell the freesias
as I slowly walk the hills

or sit by the turning mill
and sip on a wine

I'll have time to scan the trees
for koalas curled in branches
        or watch the wattlebirds
blackbirds and stately currawong
as they feed from my garden

        I'll have time to chat with Vic
whose language is coloured blue
        but whose heart is coloured gold

and I can watch the man
with the long white beard
        who is a bit of an enigma
as he sits in his armchair
        on the grass verge across the road
            from his house

yes Bridgewater
you are my kind of town

Acknowledgements

Some of these poems have been published in the following journals and anthologies:
Friendly St Reader, The Mozzie, Artstate, Elastic Time, Studio, Adelaide Independent Weekly, Common Ground No. 2, *First Refuge*, Friendly St website, *Garden Delights, Shape of My Life*.

Special thanks to Louise Nicholas for help with editing and her enthusiastic encouragement.

Thanks to Belinda Broughton for her artwork on the cover.

Thanks to my friends and fellow Hills Poets for listening to some of these poems and just being there.

Thanks also to Friendly St and First Draft
who have been supportive for many years,
and to Zenda Vecchio's reading group
who I've known for a short while
but who have shown me great encouragement.

www.ingramcontent.com/pod-product-compliance
Lightning Source LLC
Chambersburg PA
CBHW070942080526
44589CB00013B/1607